Walking the Camino de Santiago

A Journey of Faith, Discovery, and Transformation

Eric Jacobs

Book Content

Chapter 1: The Call to the Camino

Introduction to the Camino de Santiago
What inspired my pilgrimage
Preparations and planning

Chapter 2: The Way of St. James

History and significance of the pilgrimage
Different Camino routes and their characteristics
Camino Francés
Camino Portugués:

Chapter 3: Setting Off on the Journey

Departure from your starting point
First steps on the Camino

Chapter 4: Daily Life on the Trail

A day in the life of a Camino pilgrim
Albergues, refugios, and accommodations

Chapter 5: The People You Meet

Fellow pilgrims and their stories
The camaraderie of the Camino

Chapter 6: Challenges and Triumphs

Physical and mental challenges on the pilgrimage
Overcoming obstacles and finding inner strength

Chapter 7: Spiritual Reflection

The spiritual aspect of the Camino
Personal growth and self-discovery

Chapter 8: The Beauty of the Camino

The natural and cultural wonders along the way

Chapter 9: Culmination and Reflection

Reaching the Cathedral of Santiago de Compostela
Personal transformation and lessons learned

Chapter 10: Life After the Camino

Returning home and readjusting
How the Camino experience continues to influence your life

Chapter 11: Practical Tips and Resources

Advice for future pilgrims

Chapter 12: Itinerary in Camino

14 days itinerary in Camino Francés

14 day Itinerary in Camino Portugués
14 days itinerary in Camino del Norte
14 days itinerary in the Camino Primitivo

Chapter 1:

The Call to the Camino

Introduction to the Camino de Santiago

The Camino de Santiago, often known as "The Camino," is a centuries-old pilgrimage route that captivates travelers from various backgrounds. This transformative journey spans Spain and other European countries, leading pilgrims to the revered Cathedral of Santiago de Compostela, believed to be St. James's final resting place.

The Camino's allure lies not only in its historical and religious importance but also in the diverse motivations driving people worldwide to undertake this transformative venture. While some embark for religious reasons, others seek self-discovery, adventure, or a deeper connection with nature.

Offering various routes, the Camino Francés is the most popular, alongside the Camino del Norte, Camino Portugués, and more, catering to a range of pilgrims. Pilgrims encounter charming villages, historic towns, and stunning landscapes, guided by the iconic scallop shell symbolizing the converging routes to Santiago de Compostela.

This pilgrimage is not just a physical journey; it's a profound inner exploration. The challenges, camaraderie, and simplicity of trail life contribute to spiritual awakening and self-reflection.

The Camino de Santiago has a rich Middle Ages history, initiated by the discovery of St. James's relics. The "Credencial del Peregrino," a pilgrim's passport stamped along the route, is a longstanding tradition, qualifying pilgrims for a completion certificate.

The Camino emphasizes the journey over the destination, fostering simplicity and detachment. Pilgrims, carrying essentials, share meals and stories, forging a community regardless of backgrounds. The diverse landscape, from lush hills to arid plains, provides a dynamic backdrop, fostering self-discovery and personal growth away from modern distractions.

This pilgrimage is an adventure, challenging physical limits, and inviting exploration of the soul. Whether driven by faith, curiosity, or a quest for personal transformation, the Camino de Santiago promises a unique and profound journey awaiting those ready to answer its call.

What inspired my pilgrimage

In the quiet sanctuary of my quaint bookshop, where the aroma of well-worn pages mingles with the promise of undiscovered tales, fate led me to a weathered manuscript detailing a transformative pilgrimage along the Camino de Santiago. The narrative unfolded like a whispered secret, beckoning me into a world of ancient paths and profound self-discovery.

Surrounded by the embrace of familiar books, I found an inexplicable connection to the spirit of adventure and exploration within those pages. The desire to embark on a pilgrimage, not just across geographical landscapes but through the corridors of my own soul, stirred within me. The characters in the stories became my comrades, and the tales of self-discovery resonated with the unspoken yearnings of my heart.

In the ensuing months, my life mirrored the ebb and flow of a pilgrimage. The patrons entering my bookstore weren't merely customers; they were kindred spirits on their unique journeys. Each shared story, every hushed dream, fueled my growing yearning for connection and a deeper understanding of myself.

Fueled by the call of the Camino, I envisioned my pilgrimage as a symbolic quest—a personal odyssey to unveil the layers of my own existence. With a well-worn backpack slung over my shoulder and a heart pulsating with anticipation, I set forth on the ancient pathways, guided by the echoes of those who had walked before me.

The rhythmic cadence of my footsteps echoed the beats of my own journey toward self-discovery. Along the Camino, I encountered fellow wanderers with diverse stories etched into the soles of their shoes. In shared moments and conversations, bonds were forged that transcended language, weaving a tapestry of human connection.

As the sun dipped below the horizon, casting a warm glow on the final stretch of my pilgrimage, I arrived at the revered grounds of Santiago de Compostela. The cathedral loomed before me, a silent witness to the stories of countless pilgrims. With a heart overflowing with gratitude, I realized that the true inspiration behind my journey was the timeless call to explore the depths of my own existence and to walk in harmony with the world around me. The Camino, with its simple but profound moments, became my guide in discovering the beauty of my own narrative.

Preparations and planning

The Camino de Santiago, also known as the Way of St. James, is a revered pilgrimage route that spans across Spain, attracting thousands of pilgrims each year. Embarking on this spiritual journey requires careful preparation and planning. Here's a detailed guide to help you get ready for the Camino Pilgrimage:

Research and Choose Your Route: There are multiple Camino routes, each offering a unique experience. Research the different paths, considering factors like distance, difficulty, and scenery. Popular routes include the Camino Francés, Camino Portugués, and Camino del Norte.

Physical Preparation: Start a fitness regimen well in advance. Focus on cardiovascular exercises, strength training, and long walks to condition your body for the daily distances you'll cover. Break-in your hiking boots to prevent blisters during the pilgrimage.

Gear and Packing: Invest in lightweight, moisture-wicking clothing suitable for various weather conditions. Pack a good quality, comfortable backpack with essentials like a sleeping bag, quick-dry towel, toiletries, and a first aid kit.

Keep your pack's weight manageable to avoid unnecessary strain during the journey.

Accommodation: Decide whether you'll stay in albergues (hostels), hotels, or a mix of both. Book accommodations in advance during peak seasons. Consider obtaining a pilgrim passport, as it may grant you access to specific hostels and serve as a record of your journey.

Budgeting: Create a budget covering accommodation, meals, gear, and unforeseen expenses. The Camino can be affordable, but planning financially is crucial.

Language Skills: While English is widely understood, learning basic Spanish phrases can enhance your experience and interactions with locals.

Health Precautions: Visit your healthcare provider for a thorough check-up before the pilgrimage. Carry necessary medications and be aware of medical facilities along your chosen route.

Cultural Sensitivity: Familiarize yourself with the cultural norms and etiquette of the regions you'll traverse. Respect local traditions and fellow pilgrims on the journey.

Spiritual Preparation: Reflect on the spiritual aspect of the pilgrimage. Whether religious or personal, establish your intentions for the journey. Bring a small memento or token to leave at the Cruz de Ferro, a traditional symbolic act on the Camino

Navigation and Maps: Utilize guidebooks, online resources, or mobile apps to plan your daily stages. Familiarize yourself with Camino trail markers, indicating the correct path.

Flexibility and Mindset:Embrace flexibility in your schedule. Unexpected events may alter your plans, and the ability to adapt is key.
Maintain a positive mindset, as the Camino is not just a physical but also a mental challenge.

Post-Camino Reflection: Plan some time after completing the pilgrimage to reflect on your journey. Consider participating in traditional pilgrim rituals like receiving the Compostela certificate in Santiago de Compostela.

By thoroughly preparing and planning, you'll enhance your Camino experience, allowing you to fully immerse yourself in the rich history and spirituality of this ancient pilgrimage. Buen Camino!

Chapter 2:

The Way of St. James

History and significance of the pilgrimage

Pilgrimage has a rich history across various cultures and religions, with its roots deeply embedded in the human experience. The practice of embarking on a journey to a sacred or significant destination holds immense cultural, spiritual, and social significance.

Historically, pilgrimage can be traced back to ancient civilizations. In ancient Greece, individuals undertook pilgrimages to visit oracles and temples, seeking divine guidance. In Hinduism, the concept of "Tirtha Yatra" involves traveling to sacred places, often along the banks of holy rivers. In the Judeo-Christian tradition, pilgrimage has been significant, with Jerusalem being a central destination for Christians and Jews alike.

One of the most iconic pilgrimage routes is the Camino de Santiago in Spain, dating back to the Middle Ages. Pilgrims from various parts of Europe traveled to the Santiago de Compostela Cathedral, believed to house the remains of St. James. This pilgrimage became a unifying cultural and religious experience, fostering a sense of community among diverse participants.

In Islam, the Hajj pilgrimage to Mecca is one of the Five Pillars and is obligatory for every able-bodied Muslim at least once in their lifetime. This pilgrimage not only symbolizes unity among Muslims but also emphasizes equality and humility before God.

The significance of pilgrimage extends beyond religious boundaries. Many indigenous cultures have traditional pilgrimage routes, often connected to natural landmarks or ancestral sites. These journeys serve as a means of connecting with the land, ancestors, and spiritual forces.

Pilgrimage has social and psychological dimensions as well. It provides a structured way for individuals to reflect, seek spiritual growth, and experience a sense of renewal. The physical challenges and sacrifices made during a pilgrimage often contribute to a deepened sense of commitment and connection to one's faith or beliefs.

In contemporary times, pilgrimage continues to thrive, adapting to technological and societal changes. Modern transportation has made it easier for people to undertake long journeys to sacred sites. Moreover, pilgrimage has gained a secular dimension, with individuals seeking meaningful experiences beyond traditional religious contexts.

The act of pilgrimage has evolved over time, reflecting changes in religious, social, and cultural landscapes. During the medieval period in Europe, for example, pilgrimage was not only a religious practice but also a form of social and economic exchange. Pilgrimage sites became centers of commerce, with towns developing around them to accommodate and cater to the needs of the pilgrims.

In the context of Christianity, the Canterbury Tales by Geoffrey Chaucer is a literary work that vividly portrays the diverse motivations and experiences of pilgrims journeying to the shrine of Thomas Becket at Canterbury Cathedral. This narrative provides insights into the social dynamics, motivations, and challenges faced by pilgrims, emphasizing the heterogeneous nature of pilgrimage communities.

The Renaissance saw a shift in the perception of pilgrimage as humanism and a renewed interest in classical learning emerged. Pilgrimage continued, but with a greater emphasis on personal spiritual development and cultural exploration. Grand tours undertaken by the European elite during the 17th and

18th centuries can be seen as secularized forms of pilgrimage, emphasizing education, exposure to art and culture, and personal development.

In the 19th century, with the rise of industrialization and urbanization, pilgrimage experienced a decline in some regions as societal structures and values shifted. However, this period also witnessed the resurgence of interest in historical and cultural heritage, leading to the preservation and restoration of many pilgrimage sites.

The 20th century brought new dimensions to pilgrimage. The globalized world made it easier for people from different continents to undertake journeys to sacred sites, fostering intercultural exchanges. Additionally, pilgrimage became a focus for the burgeoning field of religious tourism, blending spiritual exploration with leisure and recreation.

In recent decades, pilgrimage has taken on new forms, including virtual pilgrimages facilitated by technology. People can now experience sacred sites through virtual tours, connecting with the spiritual essence of a place without physically being there. This evolution raises questions about the nature of pilgrimage in a digital age and its impact on traditional practices.

Despite these changes, the fundamental elements of pilgrimage endure. The search for meaning, self-discovery, and connection to something larger than oneself remains at the core of the pilgrimage experience. Whether undertaken for religious, cultural, or personal reasons, pilgrimage continues to be a dynamic and evolving phenomenon that reflects the intricate tapestry of human beliefs, aspirations, and the quest for transcendence.

Different Camino routes and their characteristics

The Camino de Santiago, or the Way of St. James, is a network of pilgrimage routes leading to the shrine of the apostle St. James the Great in the Cathedral of Santiago de Compostela in Galicia, northwest Spain. Here are some of the main Camino routes, each offering a unique experience:

Camino Francés: Description: The most popular and traditional route, starting in St. Jean Pied de Port in France and spanning approximately 800 km.
Characteristics: Diverse landscapes, from the Pyrenees mountains to the flat plains of Castilla, charming medieval villages, and iconic landmarks like Cruz de Ferro and the Cathedral of Santiago.

Camino del Norte: Description: Follows the northern coast of Spain, offering breathtaking coastal views.
Characteristics: Cooler and greener landscapes, challenging terrains, and a quieter atmosphere compared to the Camino Francés.

Camino Portugués: Description: Begins in Lisbon or Porto, Portugal, with various routes merging towards Santiago.

Characteristics: Rich cultural heritage, scenic coastal sections, and a more relaxed pace, making it a popular choice for those seeking a less crowded pilgrimage.

Camino Primitivo: Description: Known as the Original Way, starting in Oviedo and rejoining the Camino Francés in Melide.

Characteristics: A challenging route with mountainous terrain, beautiful landscapes, and fewer pilgrims, providing a more intimate experience.

Via de la Plata:Description: Originating in Seville, this route passes through the historic region of Extremadura.

Characteristics: Vast and varied landscapes, including rolling hills and wide plains, fewer amenities, and a sense of solitude on the trail.

Camino Inglés: Description: Historically used by pilgrims arriving by sea to A Coruña or Ferrol.

Characteristics: Shorter than other routes, diverse landscapes, and a coastal atmosphere, making it suitable for those with limited time.

Camino Finisterre: Description: An extension of the Camino Francés, leading to the "End of the Earth" at Cape Finisterre. Characteristics: Symbolic endpoint, stunning coastal views, and a sense of closure or reflection for pilgrims.

Camino del Salvador: Characteristics: Starting in León, this lesser-known route is a short but challenging option, approximately 120 kilometers long. It takes pilgrims through the mountainous terrain of Asturias before joining the Camino Francés. Highlights: The picturesque town of Pola de Lena, the mountain landscapes, and the historic Cathedral of León.

Camino Mozárabe: Characteristics: Originating in Almería or Málaga, this route winds through Andalusia before merging with the Via de la Plata. It covers around 1,000 kilometers, offering a mix of desert landscapes, olive groves, and historic towns.
Highlights: The Alhambra in Granada, the Mezquita in Córdoba, and the charming town of Mérida.

Camino de Finisterre: Characteristics: An extension of the Camino Francés, pilgrims continue from Santiago de Compostela to Cape Finisterre on the Atlantic coast. This symbolic route is about 90 kilometers long and provides a sense of closure to the pilgrimage. Highlights: The "end of the world" at Cape Finisterre, the Fisterra lighthouse, and the rugged coastal scenery.

Camino Invierno: Characteristics: Starting in Ponferrada, this winter route offers a quieter alternative to the Camino Francés. It takes pilgrims through the snowy landscapes of the Bierzo region, covering approximately 260 kilometers.
Highlights: The Templar Castle in Ponferrada, the hot springs in Ourense, and the vineyards of Ribeira Sacra.

Camino de San Olav: Characteristics: Originating in Oslo, Norway, this lesser-known route connects with the Camino Francés in Burgos. Pilgrims cover a substantial distance of around 1,500 kilometers, passing through the Scandinavian countryside and European cities.
Highlights: The Nidaros Cathedral in Trondheim, the Scandinavian landscapes, and the historic city of Burgos.

Camino del Aragones: Characteristics: Starting in the town of Somport on the French-Spanish border, this route crosses the Pyrenees and joins the Camino Francés in Puente la Reina. It covers about 160 kilometers, offering stunning mountainous landscapes. Highlights:

The medieval town of Jaca, the Monastery of San Juan de la Peña, and the picturesque town of Puente la Reina.

Camino Lebaniego: Characteristics: Beginning in the town of San Vicente de la Barquera, this route leads to the Monastery of Santo Toribio de Liébana. Pilgrims cover approximately 70 kilometers, experiencing the beauty of the Cantabrian landscapes. Highlights: The coastal town of San Vicente de la Barquera and the Monastery of Santo Toribio de Liébana.

Camino de Madrid: Characteristics: Starting in Madrid, this route spans about 320 kilometers and merges with the Camino Francés in Sahagún. Pilgrims encounter a mix of urban and rural landscapes, passing through historical towns and picturesque countryside.
Highlights: The vibrant city of Madrid, the medieval town of Segovia, and the plains of Castilla y León.

Camino de Uclés: Characteristics: Beginning in the town of Cuenca, this route leads to the Sanctuary of Uclés. Covering around 140 kilometers, it provides a unique pilgrimage experience through the Spanish interior.

Highlights: The UNESCO World Heritage Site of Cuenca, the picturesque landscapes of Castilla-La Mancha, and the Sanctuary of Uclés.

Camino de Ronda: Characteristics: A coastal route starting in the French town of Collioure and continuing along the Mediterranean coast, passing through picturesque seaside towns. It covers around 220 kilometers, offering stunning sea views.
Highlights: Collioure's coastal charm, the fishing village of Banyuls-sur-Mer, and the coastal landscapes of the Costa Brava.

Camino de la Lana: Characteristics: Beginning in Alicante, this route traverses the interior of Spain, covering about 650 kilometers. Pilgrims experience rural landscapes, vineyards, and historic towns.
Highlights: The historic town of Almansa, the vineyards of La Mancha, and the medieval city of Cuenca.

These Camino routes offer a diverse range of experiences, allowing pilgrims to choose a path that aligns with their preferences for scenery, distance, and cultural exploration. Each route has its own unique charm, making the Camino de Santiago a pilgrimage with options for every type of adventurer.

Camino Francés

The Camino Francés is not just a pilgrimage; it's a cultural and historical journey with numerous hidden gems waiting to be explored. Here's a detailed guide on things to do and how to discover the hidden treasures along the Camino Francés:

Explore St. Jean Pied de Port: Begin your journey in this picturesque French town, known for its medieval charm. Walk through its cobbled streets, visit the Citadel, and take in the stunning views of the Pyrenees.

Pamplona's Bull Run: If you're walking the Camino in July, don't miss the San Fermín festival in Pamplona. Experience the thrill of the famous Running of the Bulls.

Cultural Immersion in Burgos: Visit the UNESCO-listed Burgos Cathedral, a masterpiece of Gothic architecture. Explore the historic city center and enjoy local cuisine in one of its many tapas bars.

Meseta Experience: Embrace the beauty of the vast Meseta, a high plateau with expansive landscapes.

Discover hidden villages like Hornillos del Camino and appreciate the simplicity and serenity of rural life.

Leon's Gothic Marvels: Explore the city of Leon, home to the stunning Gothic Cathedral and the Basilica of San Isidoro. The city's rich history is reflected in its architecture and museums.

Cruz de Ferro Ritual:Take part in the pilgrim tradition at Cruz de Ferro, where travelers leave a stone symbolizing their burdens. The site offers a profound and reflective moment on the journey.

Wine Tasting in La Rioja: As you enter the La Rioja region, indulge in wine tasting. Visit local vineyards, try regional wines, and savor the flavors of this renowned wine-producing area.
Discovering Hidden Gems:

Off-the-Beaten-Path Villages: Venture off the main trail to discover charming, lesser-known villages. Places like El Acebo or Cacabelos offer a more authentic and tranquil Camino experience.
Monasteries and Convents: Seek out hidden monasteries and convents along the route. Places like San Juan de Ortega or Samos offer a peaceful retreat and a glimpse into centuries-old traditions.

Ancient Roman Ruins: Explore the Romanesque architecture and ruins along the route. Ruins near Astorga and Molinaseca provide a glimpse into the region's ancient history.

Natural Wonders: Take detours to natural wonders like Fervenza waterfall near Portomarín or the O'Cebreiro mountain pass. These hidden gems showcase the diverse landscapes of the Camino.

Local Festivals and Traditions: Research local festivals and traditions happening along the route. Participating in these events provides a unique insight into the cultural tapestry of the Camino.

Connect with Locals: Engage with locals in smaller towns and villages. This personal interaction often leads to discovering hidden gems, from local eateries to lesser-known historical sites.

The Camino Francés is not just a physical journey; it's an opportunity to immerse yourself in the rich tapestry of Spanish history, culture, and natural beauty. By exploring off the beaten path and embracing the unexpected, you'll uncover the hidden gems that make the Camino a truly transformative experience.

Camino Portugués

The Camino Portugués is a beautiful pilgrimage route that stretches from Portugal to Santiago de Compostela in Spain. Here's a detailed guide on things to do and how to explore hidden gems along the Camino Portugués:

Start in Lisbon: Begin your journey in the historic city of Lisbon. Explore the iconic Belem Tower, Jerónimos Monastery, and enjoy the vibrant atmosphere of neighborhoods like Alfama.

Coastal Scenery: Walk the scenic coastal sections, particularly on the Coastal Route. Enjoy stunning views of the Atlantic Ocean, sandy beaches, and charming fishing villages like Vila do Conde.

Porto's Ribeira District: In Porto, visit the Ribeira district along the Douro River. Wander through colorful streets, taste the famous port wine, and cross the Dom Luís I Bridge for panoramic views.

Sé Cathedral in Porto: Explore Porto's Sé Cathedral, a significant religious site with a mix of architectural styles. Take time to appreciate the views from its terrace.

Historical Braga: Detour to Braga, known for its rich history. Visit the Bom Jesus do Monte Sanctuary, a baroque masterpiece with a grand staircase and beautiful gardens.

Ponte de Lima's Charm: Ponte de Lima offers a picturesque setting with its medieval bridge and charming historic center. Visit the local market and enjoy the peaceful surroundings.

Tui and Valença: Cross into Spain through Tui and explore its cathedral. Visit the fortress town of Valença with its well-preserved walls and panoramic views of the Minho River.
Discovering Hidden Gems:

Alternative Routes: Explore alternative routes, like the Spiritual Variant or the Coastal Route. These paths often lead to hidden gems and provide a different perspective on the Camino.

Celtic Hillfort of Santa Trega: Near A Guarda, take a side trip to the Celtic hillfort of Santa Trega. The archaeological site offers breathtaking views of the coastline and the River Miño.

Albariño Wine Region: Visit the Albariño wine region in Galicia. Towns like Cambados and Combarro are known for their picturesque vineyards and historic charm.

Camarinas and the Coast of Death: Explore the rugged beauty of the Coast of Death (Costa da Morte). Camariñas, known for its lace-making tradition, is a hidden gem along this wild stretch of coastline.

Muxía and Finisterre: Extend your journey to Muxía and Finisterre, coastal towns with a mystical atmosphere. Visit the Sanctuary of Virxe da Barca and witness the sunset at Cape Finisterre.

Pontevedra's Historic Center: Wander through Pontevedra's well-preserved historic center. This charming town offers quaint squares, medieval architecture, and a tranquil atmosphere.

Local Culinary Delights: Indulge in local culinary delights. Taste seafood in coastal towns, try Albariño wine, and savor regional specialties in small village eateries.

The Camino Portugués offers a diverse range of experiences, from vibrant cities to serene coastal landscapes. By exploring off the main path and being open to detours, you'll uncover the hidden gems that make this Camino a unique and memorable journey.

Chapter 3:

Setting Off on the Journey

Departure from your starting point

The air is crisp with the promise of adventure as you stand at the threshold of your journey, ready to depart from the familiar embrace of your starting point. The sun casts its golden hues across the landscape, creating a mosaic of warmth and anticipation. With a backpack laden with essentials and a heart heavy with excitement, you embark on the pilgrimage to Camino de Santiago.

The first steps echo with a symphony of mixed emotions – the thrill of the unknown, the bittersweet farewell to the comfort of routine, and the pulsating rhythm of your own heartbeat merging with the earth beneath your feet. As you traverse through quaint villages and undulating landscapes, each footfall becomes a rhythmic dance, a testament to the resilience that propels you forward.

The scenery unfolds like a carefully crafted tapestry, weaving together the rustic charm of cobblestone streets, the verdant embrace of rolling hills, and the occasional glimpse of ancient architecture that whispers tales of centuries past. The path stretches out before you, an uncharted course that beckons with the promise of self-discovery and spiritual reflection.

Amidst the serenity of nature's symphony, the rustling leaves and distant birdsong harmonize with the cadence of your footsteps, creating a melody that accompanies you on this transformative odyssey. The scent of wildflowers and the earthy aroma of the countryside envelop you, heightening your senses and grounding you in the present moment.

As the day unfolds, encounters with fellow pilgrims become threads woven into the rich fabric of your experience. Shared smiles, exchanged stories, and silent camaraderie forge connections that transcend language, binding you together in a collective pilgrimage towards a shared destination.

With each passing milestone, the weight of your backpack begins to feel lighter, mirroring the gradual shedding of the unnecessary burdens carried within. The journey becomes a metaphorical labyrinth, leading you not only towards a physical destination but also inward, unraveling layers of introspection and self-awareness.

As the sun dips below the horizon, casting a palette of warm hues across the sky, you find solace in the simplicity of a communal meal and the camaraderie of fellow travelers. The albergues, with their welcoming glow, offer shelter and a chance for weary bodies to rest, rejuvenate, and share the collective spirit of the Camino.

The following morning, as dawn paints the sky with hues of pink and gold, you resume your pilgrimage with a renewed sense of purpose. The landscape evolves, presenting a dynamic tableau that shifts from dense woodlands to open fields, mirroring the ebb and flow of your own inner journey.

The Camino, marked by iconic scallop shells and yellow arrows, serves as both guide and silent companion. Each marker signifies not only the correct path but also a reminder that countless others have trodden this sacred route, leaving behind their hopes, dreams, and footsteps etched into the very fabric of the pilgrimage.

Amidst the rhythmic footfalls and meditative solitude, the pilgrimage becomes a personal meditation. The gentle crunch of gravel beneath your boots becomes a mantra, grounding you in the present and fostering a profound connection with the Earth. It's a communion of the physical and spiritual, a dance between self and surroundings.

As you approach historic landmarks and age-old churches, a palpable sense of reverence permeates the air. The Camino de Santiago, with its rich history and spiritual significance, becomes a conduit for contemplation. Each chapel, each ancient stone, carries the weight of centuries, inviting you to pause and reflect on the passage of time and the transient nature of existence.

Encounters with locals in quaint villages add a cultural dimension to your journey. Their warm hospitality, shared stories, and the taste of traditional cuisine infuse the pilgrimage with a sense of community. The Camino, in essence, becomes a living, breathing entity—a tapestry interwoven with the threads of diverse lives converging on a singular path.

As the days unfold into weeks, fatigue and challenges become inevitable companions. Yet, it is within these moments of struggle that the true essence of the pilgrimage emerges. Each uphill climb and blistered step become metaphors for life's challenges, and every descent represents the resilience to overcome adversity.

The evenings bring a symphony of shared experiences around communal tables. Conversations flow like the local wine, transcending language barriers and cultural differences. It's a collective celebration of the human spirit, a reminder that regardless of origin or background, the Camino de Santiago unites pilgrims in a shared quest for meaning and purpose.

Finally, as the spires of Santiago de Compostela come into view, a surge of emotions envelops you—joy, accomplishment, and a hint of nostalgia for the path left behind.

The journey, both physical and spiritual, culminates in the grandeur of the cathedral, where centuries of pilgrims have stood before you, their collective energy echoing through time. With each step, you move closer to the sacred destination, but more importantly, you draw nearer to the essence of your own pilgrimage, where the path becomes a metaphor for life's journey, and every moment is a step towards self-discovery and enlightenment.

First steps on the Camino

Embarking on the Camino de Santiago is a transformative journey, marked by rich cultural experiences and personal discovery. The first steps on this pilgrimage require careful preparation and a sense of adventure. Here's a detailed guide to those initial stages:

Research and Planning: Begin by researching the different Camino routes, such as the Camino Frances, Portugues, or Norte, and choose the one that aligns with your preferences and fitness level. Plan your starting point and estimate daily walking distances based on your fitness and the time you have available.

Packing Essentials:Prioritize lightweight and moisture-wicking clothing for the varying weather conditions along the route. Include a sturdy pair of walking shoes, a comfortable backpack, and a well-fitted hat to shield yourself from the sun.

Accommodation: Decide whether you'll stay in albergues (pilgrim hostels), hotels, or a mix of both. Booking in advance may be necessary during peak seasons. Consider obtaining a pilgrim passport (Credencial) to avail of discounted rates at accommodations.

Health Preparations: Consult with a healthcare professional to ensure you're physically prepared for the journey, especially if you have any existing health concerns. Pack a basic first aid kit, including blister treatment, pain relievers, and any prescribed medications.

Cultural Etiquette: Familiarize yourself with the cultural and religious aspects of the regions you'll be passing through. Learn a few basic phrases in the local language to enhance your interactions with locals.

Travel Logistics:Arrange your transportation to the starting point of your chosen Camino route. Be mindful of the specific logistics, such as airport transfers and local transportation options.

Orientation in the Starting Town: Upon arrival, take time to explore the starting town and soak in the pre-Camino atmosphere.
Attend pilgrim orientation sessions if available, offering valuable information and a chance to connect with fellow pilgrims.
Opening Ritual:

The Camino often begins with a symbolic ritual, such as the Pilgrim's Mass in St. Jean Pied de Port on the

Camino Frances. Participate in these rituals to set the tone for your journey.
Start Walking:

The first steps symbolize the beginning of your pilgrimage. Take them with intention and mindfulness.
Pace yourself and listen to your body. It's not a race, but a personal journey with its own rhythm.
Connect with Fellow Pilgrims:

Share stories, exchange advice, and forge connections with other pilgrims. The camaraderie along the Camino is a unique and enriching aspect of the experience.
Remember, the Camino is not just a physical journey but a profound exploration of self and culture. Approach it with an open heart, and each step will bring you closer to the transformative essence of the Camino de Santiago.

Chapter 4:

Daily Life on the Trail

A day in the life of a Camino pilgrim

The day begins before sunrise, as a Camino pilgrim rises in anticipation of another day on the ancient pilgrimage route. The air is crisp, and the first rays of sunlight illuminate the picturesque landscapes that stretch out ahead. After a simple breakfast in a communal albergue, the pilgrim laces up their worn-in hiking boots and sets off.

The path unfolds through charming villages, rolling hills, and dense forests, each step a rhythmic cadence echoing centuries of pilgrimage tradition. Along the way, the pilgrim encounters fellow seekers from around the world, forging connections through shared smiles and nods. Conversations, often in a mix of languages, weave a tapestry of diverse stories and motivations.

As the sun climbs higher, the midday break beckons. Pilgrims gather in shaded spots, savoring a packed lunch of local cheese, bread, and fresh fruit. A sense of camaraderie prevails, the shared fatigue transforming into a unifying bond. After the rest, the journey resumes, and the pilgrim presses on, the kilometers ticking away beneath their determined steps.

Arriving in a historic town, the pilgrim explores narrow cobblestone streets, discovering churches, quaint cafes, and ancient landmarks. The day's physical exertion contrasts with moments of quiet introspection, as the pilgrim contemplates their reasons for walking the Camino. The pilgrimage, both a physical and spiritual endeavor, unfolds as a journey inward as much as outward.

Evenings bring the pilgrim to a communal dinner in the albergue, where stories of the day are shared over hearty meals. A sense of community deepens as tired bodies find rest in shared dormitories. Lights dim, and the rustling sounds of sleeping bags fill the air, signaling the end of another day on the Camino.

The night is both a sanctuary and a place of contemplation. The dormitory, filled with the soft sounds of fellow pilgrims breathing and shifting in their sleep, becomes a haven for rest and reflection. The worn-out boots rest by the bunk, and the pilgrim, wrapped in a cocoon of warmth, drifts into a well-earned slumber.

Dawn breaks, and the routine begins anew. The pilgrim, guided by the symbolic yellow arrows that mark the Camino, embarks on another day of challenges and discoveries. The landscape evolves—open fields give way to rocky trails, and the terrain undulates with the rhythm of the journey. Each step carries a dual purpose: a physical progression along the path and a metaphorical journey inward.

The pilgrim encounters pilgrim's milestones—a wayside cross, a medieval bridge, a chapel with a history steeped in legend. These landmarks punctuate the pilgrimage, offering moments of reflection and gratitude for the ancient traditions that have paved the way. Local villagers extend warm welcomes, their generosity leaving a lasting impression on the pilgrim's heart.

Meals become a ritual, not just for sustenance but for sharing experiences and forming bonds. The simple act of breaking bread with fellow pilgrims transforms into a celebration of unity, transcending language barriers and cultural differences. Conversations delve into life's purpose, shared dreams, and the transformative power of the journey.

As the day progresses, fatigue sets in, challenging the pilgrim's resolve. Blisters form, muscles ache, yet the pilgrimage spirit prevails. The albergue at day's end becomes a sanctuary once more, a place to tend to weary feet, launder sweat-soaked clothes, and recharge for the days ahead.

Evenings on the Camino bring a kaleidoscope of emotions. Sunset paints the sky in hues of orange and pink, casting a serene backdrop for reflections on the day's triumphs and tribulations. A communal pilgrim's mass in a historic church provides a spiritual anchor, a moment to express gratitude for the journey and seek guidance for the road ahead.

As the pilgrim drifts into sleep, beneath the canopy of stars, there's a profound awareness that each day on the Camino is not just a step closer to a destination but a transformative passage. The physical and spiritual dimensions intertwine, shaping a profound narrative of self-discovery and shared humanity along this timeless pilgrimage route.

Albergues, refugios, and accommodations

The Camino de Santiago, also known as the Way of St. James, is a network of pilgrim routes leading to the shrine of the apostle Saint James in the Cathedral of Santiago de Compostela in Galicia, northwest Spain. Along this historic pilgrimage, travelers have various accommodation options, including albergues, refugios, and other types of lodgings.

Albergues: Albergues are budget accommodations specifically designed for pilgrims on the Camino de Santiago. They are found along the entire route and provide a communal experience. Pilgrims often share dormitory-style rooms with bunk beds. These establishments are run by municipalities, private individuals, or religious institutions. Albergues typically offer basic amenities such as communal kitchens, washing facilities, and communal gathering areas. They aim to create a sense of community among pilgrims and are an affordable option for those on a budget.

Refugios: Refugios are similar to albergues and are commonly found on the Camino. The terms are often used interchangeably. Refugios provide shelter and basic facilities for pilgrims, emphasizing the communal nature of the pilgrimage experience. Pilgrims often stay in shared dormitories and have access to communal spaces.

Refugios can be managed by local associations, municipalities, or private individuals. While some are donation-based, others may have a fixed fee for accommodation.

Other Accommodations: Apart from albergues and refugios, pilgrims on the Camino de Santiago can choose from a variety of other accommodations to suit their preferences and budget. These include hostels, guesthouses, hotels, and even monasteries. Hostels and guesthouses offer a more private and comfortable stay, often with private rooms and additional amenities. Hotels provide a higher level of comfort and luxury, catering to those who prefer a more upscale experience. Monasteries along the route also offer a unique opportunity for pilgrims to experience a stay in a spiritual setting.

Booking and Availability: It's advisable for pilgrims to plan their accommodations in advance, especially during peak seasons when the Camino is more crowded. Many albergues and accommodations allow reservations, while others operate on a first-come, first-served basis. Pilgrims should consider their daily walking distance, health, and preferences when choosing accommodations.

The Camino de Santiago offers a diverse range of accommodations, from communal albergues and refugios to more private hostels, guesthouses, and hotels. The choice depends on the pilgrim's preferences, budget, and the kind of experience they seek on this historic and transformative journey.

Chapter 5:

The People You Meet

Fellow pilgrims and their stories

On a pilgrimage, the journey often intertwines with the diverse stories of fellow travelers, creating a tapestry of experiences and connections. As you embark on this spiritual or cultural quest, you encounter a myriad of people, each with a unique narrative that adds depth to the pilgrimage.

Shared Devotion: Pilgrims often share a common purpose, be it a religious devotion or a quest for personal enlightenment. The shared commitment to this purpose fosters a sense of camaraderie among the pilgrims, creating a supportive community on the journey.

Cultural Exchange: Pilgrimages attract individuals from various cultural backgrounds, contributing to a rich tapestry of diversity. Conversations with fellow pilgrims become a cultural exchange, offering insights into different traditions, customs, and beliefs, fostering a deeper understanding of humanity's varied perspectives.

Personal Transformation Stories: Many pilgrims embark on their journey seeking personal transformation. The people you meet may share tales of profound changes, whether overcoming personal challenges, finding inner peace, or experiencing spiritual awakenings. These stories inspire and resonate, adding an emotional layer to the pilgrimage.

Interconnected Paths: Pilgrimages often follow well-trodden paths, where the stories of those who came before intertwine with the present journey. Learning about the experiences of those who walked the same path in the past can create a sense of continuity, connecting you to a broader, historical narrative.

Acts of Kindness: The pilgrimage journey is marked by acts of kindness and mutual support among pilgrims. Strangers become friends as they share resources, offer assistance, and provide encouragement. These moments of human connection exemplify the communal spirit that permeates the pilgrimage experience.

Challenges and Triumphs: Pilgrimages are not without challenges. The people you meet will likely have faced obstacles and triumphs along the way. Hearing about their struggles and victories adds a realistic dimension to the pilgrimage, emphasizing the resilience of the human spirit.

Unexpected Connections: Some of the most profound interactions on a pilgrimage come from unexpected encounters. A brief conversation with a fellow pilgrim may lead to insights, friendships, or collaborations that enrich the overall experience, demonstrating the serendipity embedded in the journey.

Varied Perspectives on Faith: Pilgrims often approach their spiritual journey with unique perspectives on faith. Conversations with fellow travelers reveal a spectrum of beliefs, interpretations, and personal connections to the sacred, fostering a nuanced understanding of spirituality that transcends cultural boundaries.

Cross-Generational Bonds: Pilgrimages draw people of different ages and life stages. Interactions between generations create a dynamic blend of wisdom-sharing and youthful enthusiasm, forming bonds that bridge generational gaps and contribute to the collective wisdom of the pilgrimage community.

Solo Pilgrims: Amidst the group dynamics, you may encounter solo pilgrims pursuing their spiritual or personal quests independently. Their stories often reflect a profound sense of self-discovery and resilience, showcasing the capacity for individual growth within the communal context of the pilgrimage.

Local Guides and Residents: Beyond fellow pilgrims, interactions with local guides and residents along the route add another layer to the narrative. Their stories provide insights into the significance of the pilgrimage site, local traditions, and the impact of pilgrims on the communities they pass through.

Reflection and Contemplation: The people you meet may share moments of deep reflection and contemplation. Whether in group discussions, quiet moments of solitude, or shared rituals, these interactions contribute to the overall introspective nature of the pilgrimage, emphasizing the personal and collective journey within.

Celebration of Diversity: Pilgrimages celebrate the diversity of human experiences. Through the stories of fellow pilgrims, you witness the tapestry of humanity with its joys, sorrows, challenges, and celebrations. This celebration of diversity becomes a unifying force, transcending differences and fostering a sense of global interconnectedness.

Legacy of Legends: Some pilgrimages are associated with legendary figures or historical events. Fellow pilgrims may share anecdotes and folklore related to these legends, breathing life into the mythical aspects of the journey and connecting you to a narrative that transcends time.

Continued Connections: The connections forged during a pilgrimage often extend beyond the journey's conclusion. Pilgrims may choose to stay in touch, creating a network of like-minded individuals who share a bond forged through the transformative experience of pilgrimage.

The people encountered during a pilgrimage contribute to a multifaceted narrative, encompassing spirituality, culture, personal growth, and the intricate threads of human connection. Their stories become an integral part of the pilgrimage's lasting impact on individual lives and the collective memory of the sacred journey.

The camaraderie of the Camino

The Camino de Santiago, often referred to as the Way of St. James, is a network of pilgrimage routes leading to the shrine of the apostle Saint James the Great in the Cathedral of Santiago de Compostela in Galicia, northwest Spain. Beyond its religious significance, the Camino is renowned for fostering a unique camaraderie among pilgrims.

Pilgrims, irrespective of nationality, age, or background, embark on this transformative journey for various reasons – spiritual growth, self-discovery, or simply the challenge of the trek. What makes the Camino special is the sense of unity that emerges along the path. Strangers become companions, connected by a shared purpose and the shared experience of navigating the trail's physical and emotional challenges.

The trek's arduous nature strips away superficial differences, creating an environment where genuine connections can flourish. Pilgrims often share meals, stories, and even walking companionship, forming bonds that transcend language barriers and cultural divides. This spontaneous sense of community is a testament to the Camino's ability to dissolve societal boundaries and foster a universal human connection.

The albergues, or pilgrim hostels, where trekkers rest each night, play a pivotal role in nurturing this camaraderie. Shared dormitories and communal spaces encourage interaction, and pilgrims engage in conversations that range from personal reflections to cultural exchanges. The collective fatigue and common goal create an atmosphere where empathy and support thrive, turning strangers into friends and sometimes lifelong companions.

The symbolic act of carrying a scallop shell, the emblem of the Camino, further unifies pilgrims. The shell serves both as a wayfinding marker and a symbol of pilgrimage, fostering a sense of identity and solidarity among those on the journey. The shared rituals, such as receiving stamps in the pilgrim's passport (Credencial) at designated stops, also contribute to a communal spirit, reinforcing the idea that everyone is part of a larger, shared narrative.

As pilgrims reach Santiago de Compostela, the destination of their arduous trek, the sense of camaraderie reaches its pinnacle. The joy of accomplishment is magnified by the shared experiences along the way. Pilgrims gather in the cathedral square, often emotional and reflective, celebrating not only reaching the physical endpoint but also the bonds forged with fellow trekkers.

The camaraderie of the Camino de Santiago is a testament to the human spirit's capacity for connection and compassion. The shared challenges, mutual support, and the universal quest for meaning create a unique social tapestry that enriches the pilgrimage experience. Beyond the physical journey, it is the relationships built along the way that make the Camino a transformative and enduring memory for those who undertake its path.

Chapter 6:

Challenges and Triumphs

Physical and mental challenges on the pilgrimage

Embarking on a pilgrimage is a profound journey that often involves a combination of physical and mental challenges. These challenges can vary depending on the specific pilgrimage route and individual circumstances, but there are common threads that many pilgrims encounter.

Physical Challenges:

Long Distances: Pilgrimages often cover extensive distances, requiring participants to walk or travel for extended periods. The physical strain of walking long distances can lead to fatigue, blisters, and muscle soreness.

Harsh Terrain: Pilgrimage routes may traverse diverse landscapes, including mountains, deserts, and uneven terrain. Pilgrims must navigate challenging conditions such as steep ascents and descents, rocky paths, and inclement weather, adding an extra layer of difficulty.

Weather Conditions: Pilgrims may face extreme weather conditions, ranging from scorching heat to freezing cold, depending on the time of year and location. This can affect physical well-being and necessitate careful preparation.

Accommodation and Facilities: Basic living conditions during a pilgrimage, such as shared accommodations and limited amenities, can pose physical discomfort and challenges. Pilgrims may need to adapt to simple living arrangements and communal facilities.

Health Concerns: Pilgrims may face health issues such as dehydration, exhaustion, and even altitude sickness in mountainous regions. Access to medical facilities may be limited, intensifying the importance of maintaining good health throughout the journey.

Weight of Belongings: Carrying backpacks or other belongings for an extended period can strain the back and shoulders. Pilgrims often need to strike a balance between carrying essential items and minimizing the physical burden on their bodies.

Footwear and Clothing: Inappropriate footwear can lead to foot problems, and the choice of clothing is crucial in extreme weather conditions. Pilgrims must carefully select their attire to ensure comfort and protection against the elements

Mental Challenges:

Isolation and Solitude: Pilgrimages often involve periods of solitude, providing individuals with ample time for self-reflection. However, this isolation can also be mentally challenging, leading to feelings of loneliness or introspective discomfort.

Spiritual Struggle: Pilgrimages are inherently spiritual journeys, and participants may grapple with profound existential questions or encounter moments of doubt about their beliefs. This inner conflict can be mentally taxing.

Cultural Adjustment: Pilgrims often encounter diverse cultures and customs along their route. Adapting to new environments, languages, and social norms can be mentally challenging, requiring openness and flexibility.

Emotional Release: The intense nature of pilgrimages can bring about a range of emotions, from deep spiritual connection to moments of frustration or sadness. Pilgrims may face emotional challenges as they confront aspects of their lives and beliefs.

Goal Alignment: Setting and achieving spiritual or personal goals during a pilgrimage can be mentally demanding. Striving for self-discovery or seeking answers to existential questions requires mental resilience and determination.

Social Dynamics: Pilgrims often find themselves in diverse groups or communities, and navigating social interactions can be challenging. Differences in languages, backgrounds, and personalities can contribute to both enriching experiences and moments of tension.

Coping with Uncertainty: Pilgrimages are inherently unpredictable, and unforeseen circumstances such as route changes or logistical challenges can create stress. Pilgrims must learn to adapt to the unexpected and maintain a positive mindset in the face of uncertainty.

Time Away from Routine: The disruption of one's usual routine during a pilgrimage can be mentally challenging. Pilgrims may need to reconcile with the absence of familiar comforts, routines, and the demands of daily life, leading to a period of adjustment.

Cultural Sensitivity: Engaging with diverse cultures along the pilgrimage route requires a high degree of cultural sensitivity. Misunderstandings or unintentional cultural faux pas can create moments of discomfort, emphasizing the importance of open-mindedness and respect.

Post-Pilgrimage Integration: Returning to everyday life after a transformative pilgrimage can be mentally challenging. Pilgrims may grapple with integrating the lessons learned and experiences gained into their regular routines, finding a balance between the sacred journey and the demands of the modern world.

The physical and mental challenges of a pilgrimage contribute to the transformative nature of the journey. Pilgrims often find that overcoming these obstacles fosters personal growth, resilience, and a deeper connection to the spiritual or cultural significance of their pilgrimage.

Setting out on the Camino de Santiago journey frequently includes confronting physical, profound, and otherworldly hindrances. The excursion turns into a representation for life's difficulties, and conquering them requires taking advantage of one's internal strength.

Actual Difficulties: The burdensome journey through fluctuating territories can test one's actual perseverance. Rankled feet, sore muscles, and fatigue become normal buddies. However, each forward-moving step turns into a demonstration of strength and assurance, delineating the limit of the human body to adjust and survive.

Profound Choppiness: The Camino isn't simply an actual excursion however a profoundly close to home one. Isolation, experiences with different people, and snapshots of reflection can work up a scope of feelings. Facing inward feelings of dread and questions turns into a fundamental piece of the journey, preparing for close to home development.

3. Eccentric Components: Weather conditions changes, surprising diversions, and strategic difficulties are unavoidable. These interruptions force pioneers to embrace flexibility and develop persistence. The capriciousness of the excursion turns into an illustration in giving up control and confiding simultaneously.

4. Kinship and Association: Imparting the way to individual travelers cultivates a feeling of local area. The common help and shared encounters make an organization of consolation. Finding strength in solidarity, travelers discover that confronting deterrents turns out to be more reasonable when joined by others.

5. Otherworldly Reflection: The Camino gives adequate chance to reflection and otherworldly examination. Pioneers frequently wrestle with existential inquiries, looking for importance and reason. This interior investigation can prompt the disclosure of significant inward strength and versatility established in one's convictions and values.

6. Observing Little Triumphs: Finishing each phase of the excursion, beating individual restrictions, and arriving at achievements act as tokens of one's abilities. Explorers figure out how to commend the little triumphs, developing a positive mentality that adds to persevering through the difficulties that lie ahead.

7. Inward Change: As the miles gather, travelers go through a groundbreaking cycle. The difficulties confronted and defeat add to a more profound comprehension of oneself. Inward strength isn't simply an actual quality yet a significant acknowledgment of one's flexibility, perseverance, and limit with regards to development.

8. Examples from Straightforwardness: The moderate way of life on the Camino, where everyday necessities fit into a knapsack, helps explorers to see the value in straightforwardness. Stripping away material solaces empowers an emphasis on the fundamentals, featuring the internal strength got from adjusting to a less confounded lifestyle.

9. Confronting Evil presences and Fears: The isolation and intelligent nature of the Camino give an interesting an open door to stand up to individual devils and fears. Explorers discover that recognizing and testing these conflicts under the surface is fundamental for self-awareness and the advancement of inward strength.

10. Association with Nature: The Camino's picturesque scenes offer a significant association with nature. Strolling through woodlands, mountains, and rustic towns encourages a feeling of concordance and quietness. Nature turns into a wellspring of motivation and revival, adding to the otherworldly and close to home versatility of the traveler.

11. Confiding in Outsiders: Travelers frequently depend on the benevolence of outsiders for help, whether it's bearings, a spot to remain, or a straightforward thoughtful gesture. Confiding in the intrinsic decency of others turns into a strong example, building up the possibility that strength can be tracked down inside oneself as well as in the aggregate help of humankind.

12. Versatility Notwithstanding Difficulties: Experiencing mishaps, be it through actual wounds or startling difficulties, tests one's flexibility. Pioneers figure out how to quickly return from mishaps, understanding that difficulties are not barriers but rather bypasses that can in any case prompt self-awareness and self-disclosure.

13. Relinquishing Self image: The Camino urges travelers to shed inner self driven concerns and embrace lowliness. As people from different foundations merge on similar way, progressive systems disintegrate, cultivating a climate where everybody is equivalent. This shedding of self image adds to the improvement of internal strength grounded in lowliness.

14. Coordination of Brain, Body, and Soul: The actual effort of strolling, joined with snapshots of consideration, makes an integrative encounter for psyche, body, and soul. Travelers find that genuine inward strength arises from actual perseverance as well as from the arrangement and equilibrium of all features of their being.

15. Appearance and Reflection: Arriving at the excursion's end at Santiago de Compostela marks a significant snapshot of reflection. Explorers think back on the difficulties confronted, the inward strength found, and the individual changes gone through. This appearance fills in as a representative zenith of the journey's examples and a demonstration of the persevering through force of the human soul.

Fundamentally, the Camino de Santiago journey fills in as a microcosm of life's excursion. Conquering impediments and finding inward strength on this way mirrors the general human experience of flexibility, self-disclosure, and the nonstop quest for self-improvement.

Chapter 7:

Spiritual Reflection

The spiritual aspect of the Camino

The Camino de Santiago, a prestigious journey course, rises above its actual excursion, digging profound into the domains of otherworldly reflection. Pioneers set out on this old way not exclusively to cross the pleasant scenes yet additionally to associate with their internal identities and investigate the otherworldly components of their lives.

As walkers cross the different territories of the Camino, they frequently wind up in a pensive state. The musical rhythm of strides turns into a reflective work on, cultivating contemplation and self-revelation. The isolation of the excursion gives a remarkable open door to explorers to detach from the interruptions of current life and tune into their profound quintessence.

Along the Camino, there are markers of significant profound importance. Pioneers experience holy locales, places of worship, and landmarks that convey hundreds of years of history and profound energy. These spots act as impetuses for profound reflection, inciting explorers to consider their convictions, values, and life's motivation.

Meeting individual pioneers from different foundations and societies adds a common aspect to the otherworldly experience. Shared stories, shared help, and the aggregate quest for a shared objective make a feeling of solidarity and interconnectedness. The Camino turns into a microcosm of the human excursion, mirroring the different ways individuals take throughout everyday life and the common mission for importance.

The effortlessness of pioneer life, with its emphasis on essential necessities and a conscious separation from material solaces, cultivates a feeling of otherworldly gravity. Deprived of overabundance, travelers frequently find that the fundamentals of life become more obvious, prompting an elevated consciousness of appreciation, modesty, and the interconnectedness, everything being equal.

The actual difficulties of the Camino likewise assume a part in the otherworldly reflection process. Getting through lengthy strolls, confronting weariness, and defeating hindrances become analogies for life's battles. Explorers draw strength from these difficulties, perceiving that the actual excursion is extraordinary, reflecting the highs and lows of their own and profound development.

The otherworldly reflection on the Camino stretches out past the actual way, venturing into the domain of care and presence. The tedious idea of strolling, combined with the straightforwardness of the day to day daily schedule, urges travelers to be completely present in every second. This elevated mindfulness turns into a door to a more profound association with the heavenly, nature, and oneself.

Numerous pioneers view the Camino as an emblematic portrayal of life's excursion. The illustration of strolling towards an objective repeats the more extensive mission for reason and satisfaction. Each step turns into an amazing chance to shed loads, discharge the past, and embrace the present. The allegorical meaning of the excursion permits travelers to see difficulties not as snags but rather as indispensable pieces of their own and otherworldly development.

The demonstration of strolling itself can be a type of moving reflection. As travelers track old ways, encompassed by the excellence of nature, they frequently track down comfort and motivation. The mood of strides turns into a mantra, directing them into a condition of internal tranquility. In this quietude, otherworldly bits of knowledge might arise, and a significant association with the heavenly or the universe is frequently capable.

The Camino's otherworldly charm isn't bound to a particular strict belief system. While it has profound roots in Christianity, inviting pioneers to the burial chamber of St. James in Santiago de Compostela, individuals of different religions and otherworldly convictions attempt this excursion. This inclusivity makes a rich embroidery of points of view, encouraging interfaith discourse and understanding.

The public parts of the Camino further intensify its profound aspect. Shared feasts, mutual albergues (inns), and aggregate festivals make a feeling of profound connection. That's what pioneers find, regardless of contrasts in language, culture, and foundation, there is a general string of mankind that ties them together. This common journey experience turns into a microcosm of the interconnectedness that underlies every single otherworldly custom.

The Camino de Santiago fills in as an extraordinary journey that goes past the actual test of strolling. A profound odyssey welcomes reflection, care, and association with the heavenly. Whether one looks for strict edification, self-disclosure, or a feeling of solidarity with individual pioneers, the Camino offers a sacrosanct space for significant profound reflection.

Personal growth and self-discovery

The Camino de Santiago, a centuries-old pilgrimage route, is not merely a physical journey across the stunning landscapes of Spain. It's a transformative experience that often becomes a profound catalyst for personal growth and self-discovery.

As pilgrims traverse the ancient path, they navigate not only the diverse terrain but also the inner landscapes of their minds and hearts. The simplicity of the pilgrimage, the rhythmic footsteps, and the shared camaraderie create a conducive environment for self-reflection.

The daily routine of walking, often for weeks, provides ample time for introspection. Pilgrims find themselves confronting their fears, doubts, and desires. The solitude of the trail becomes a canvas for contemplation, allowing individuals to delve into their core values and beliefs.

The Camino is a melting pot of diverse individuals, each carrying their own stories and burdens. Interactions with fellow pilgrims and the communal spirit of the journey foster empathy and understanding. This shared human experience encourages personal growth by breaking down societal barriers and fostering connections based on authenticity and vulnerability.

Moreover, the physical challenges of the Camino, be it climbing steep ascents or enduring blistering sun, mirror life's obstacles. Overcoming these hurdles fosters resilience and self-confidence. Pilgrims discover strengths they didn't know they possessed, both physically and mentally.

As the miles pass, pilgrims shed not only the weight of their backpacks but also the burdens of their past. The simplicity of daily life on the Camino allows for a detoxification of the mind from the noise and distractions of modern life. This detox paves the way for a deeper understanding of oneself and a reevaluation of life's priorities.

The symbolic act of reaching Santiago de Compostela, the pilgrimage's final destination, marks not just the end of a physical journey but the beginning of a new chapter in one's life. Pilgrims often return home with a clearer sense of purpose, a heightened appreciation for simplicity, and a profound understanding of their own capabilities.

The Camino Experience is a transformative odyssey that transcends the physical act of walking. It is a pilgrimage of the soul, a sacred journey where personal growth and self-discovery unfold step by step, echoing the sentiment that the road to self-realization is as important as the destination itself.

Chapter 8:

The Beauty of the Camino

The natural and cultural wonders along the way

The Camino de Santiago, often referred to as the Way of St. James, is a network of pilgrimage routes leading to the shrine of the apostle Saint James the Great in the Cathedral of Santiago de Compostela in Galicia, northwest Spain. Beyond its religious significance, the Camino is renowned for its profound beauty, both natural and cultural, that captivates the hearts of pilgrims and travelers alike.

1. Natural Wonders

Lush Landscapes: The Camino traverses diverse terrains, from the verdant landscapes of the Pyrenees to the sun-kissed plains of the Meseta. Pilgrims experience a visual feast of lush forests, rolling hills, and meandering rivers.

Scenic Vistas: Breathtaking viewpoints, such as the Cruz de Ferro, offer panoramic views that inspire introspection. The ever-changing scenery along the route keeps walkers engaged and amazed.

2. Historical and Cultural Riches:

Charming Villages: The Camino winds through picturesque villages frozen in time, each with its unique character and architecture. From the cobblestone streets of Santo Domingo de la Calzada to the medieval charm of Burgos, history comes alive at every step.

Architectural Marvels: Magnificent cathedrals like the one in Leon and Romanesque churches dot the route, showcasing centuries of architectural prowess. These structures stand as testament to the deep cultural and religious roots embedded in the Camino's history.

3. Local Flavors and Culinary Delights:

Gastronomic Journey: The Camino is a culinary adventure, allowing pilgrims to savor the diverse flavors of Spanish cuisine. From hearty stews in the rustic mesones to freshly caught seafood in coastal regions, each meal is a celebration of local ingredients and traditions.

Wine Regions: Passing through renowned wine regions like La Rioja, pilgrims have the opportunity to taste world-class wines. Vineyards stretch across the landscape, adding a touch of sophistication to the rustic beauty of the journey.

4. Human Connection and Spiritual Fulfillment:

Community Spirit: The Camino fosters a unique sense of camaraderie among pilgrims from all walks of life. Shared challenges and triumphs create lasting bonds, making the journey as much about the people as the path.

Spiritual Reflection: Whether motivated by faith or a personal quest for meaning, the Camino offers a space for introspection and spiritual connection. Pilgrims often find solace in the simplicity of the pilgrimage, gaining insights that transcend the physical journey.

5. Symbolism and Rituals:

The Waymarks: Yellow arrows and scallop shells guide pilgrims along the route, symbolizing the unity of all paths leading to Santiago. These waymarks not only provide practical direction but also serve as a powerful metaphor for life's journey.

Pilgrim's Passport: The issuance of a Pilgrim's Passport, stamped at various stops along the way, becomes a cherished memento. This simple document carries the weight of the miles walked and the encounters experienced, documenting the individual's unique pilgrimage.

6. Varied Camino Routes:

The French Way: Perhaps the most popular route, the Camino Francés, spans over 500 miles from St. Jean Pied de Port to Santiago. It showcases the diverse beauty of Spain, from the Pyrenees to the Galician countryside.

The Coastal Camino: Following the Atlantic coastline, this route combines the beauty of the sea with the charm of coastal villages. It provides a refreshing alternative for those seeking a different perspective on the pilgrimage.

7. Seasonal Transformations:

Spring Blooms: The Camino comes alive in spring, with wildflowers carpeting the fields and trees blossoming along the trail. The air is filled with the sweet fragrance of nature's rebirth, creating a visually stunning and uplifting atmosphere.

Autumn Colors: Fall transforms the landscape into a symphony of warm hues. The changing leaves add a layer of richness to the scenery, turning the Camino into a captivating canvas of reds, oranges, and yellows.

8. Enduring Traditions:

Pilgrim's Mass: Culminating at the Cathedral of Santiago, pilgrims attend the Pilgrim's Mass. The swinging of the Botafumeiro, a massive incense burner, is a captivating ritual that symbolizes the purification of the pilgrim's journey.

Albergues and Hospitality: The tradition of albergues, or pilgrim hostels, reflects the spirit of generosity on the Camino. Pilgrims share communal spaces, fostering a sense of mutual support and understanding.

9. Personal Transformation: Physical Challenge: The physical demands of the Camino, coupled with the mental and emotional aspects, create a transformative experience. Pilgrims often discover newfound strength and resilience within themselves.

Cathartic Release: Many walkers use the Camino as a form of catharsis, letting go of burdens and gaining clarity. The simplicity of the journey allows for introspection and personal growth.

In essence, the beauty of the Camino lies not only in its stunning landscapes and architectural wonders but also in the rich tapestry of human experiences woven into its very fabric. It is a journey that transcends the ordinary, leaving indelible memories and a profound appreciation for the natural and cultural wonders that grace this ancient pilgrimage route.

Chapter 9:

Culmination and Reflection

Reaching the Cathedral of Santiago de Compostela

Reaching the Cathedral of Santiago de Compostela is a journey that holds deep cultural and spiritual significance for pilgrims and travelers alike. The cathedral, located in the heart of Santiago de Compostela in Galicia, Spain, is the final destination of the Camino de Santiago, a network of pilgrimage routes that converge from various parts of Europe.

1. Choosing Your Camino Route: There are multiple routes to Santiago de Compostela, such as the French Way, Northern Way, and Portuguese Way. Each route

offers a unique experience, varying landscapes, and historical sites. Select the one that aligns with your preferences and time constraints.

2. Preparation: Before embarking on the pilgrimage, ensure you are physically prepared for the journey. Walking long distances daily requires stamina, so gradually increase your walking distance in the weeks leading up to your trip.

3. Accommodations: Along the Camino, you'll find a network of albergues (hostels), hotels, and guesthouses. It's advisable to plan your daily distances and book accommodations in advance, especially during peak pilgrimage seasons.

4. Navigation: Markers, known as yellow arrows and scallop shells, guide pilgrims along the Camino. Pay attention to these symbols, as well as official signage, to stay on the right path.

5. Cultural Exploration: Take the time to explore the towns and villages along the way. Each has its own charm, historical sites, and culinary specialties. Engage with locals and fellow pilgrims to enrich your cultural experience.

6. Reaching Santiago de Compostela: As you approach Santiago de Compostela, the anticipation builds. The sight of the cathedral's spires on the horizon is a powerful moment for pilgrims. Follow the scallop shells and yellow arrows into the city.

7. Pilgrim's Mass: Upon reaching the cathedral, attend the Pilgrim's Mass, a symbolic and spiritual ceremony held daily. Pilgrims receive a certificate of completion, known as the Compostela, after attending this Mass.

8. Botafumeiro Ceremony: If possible, witness the Botafumeiro ceremony, where a large censer swings

across the cathedral's nave. This centuries-old tradition adds a grandeur to the pilgrimage's conclusion.

9. Reflection and Celebration: Take time to reflect on your journey, the people you've met, and the challenges you've overcome. Celebrate your achievement with a visit to the Cathedral's rooftop for panoramic views of Santiago de Compostela.

10. Post-Camino Exploration: Santiago de Compostela itself is a captivating city with narrow streets, historic buildings, and a vibrant atmosphere. Explore the UNESCO-listed old town, visit local markets, and savor Galician cuisine.

Reaching the Cathedral of Santiago de Compostela is more than a physical journey; it's a profound experience of self-discovery, cultural immersion, and spiritual fulfillment. The pilgrimage fosters a sense of camaraderie among fellow travelers and leaves indelible memories that endure long after reaching the journey's end.

Personal transformation and lessons learned

Setting out on the Camino de Santiago is an extraordinary excursion that goes past the actual demonstration of strolling. The journey, with its old roots and otherworldly importance, offers significant illustrations that shape self-improvement. As one strolls the Camino, the way turns into a similitude forever, introducing difficulties, kinship, self-disclosure, and significant experiences.

Physical and Mental Perseverance: The Camino requests a degree of actual endurance that pushes limits. Strolling significant distances day to day tests the body as well as fortifies the brain. Getting through weariness and uneasiness cultivates strength, instructing that development frequently includes venturing outside one's usual range of familiarity.

Simplicity and Moderation: With just fundamentals conveyed in a rucksack, the Camino empowers a moderate way of life. Shedding material belongings features the freeing force of effortlessness, showing that satisfaction is found in encounters and associations as opposed to possessions.

Connection with Nature: The fluctuated scenes experienced on the Camino - from mountains to fields - offer a profound association with nature. This association cultivates appreciation for the excellence of the world and gives snapshots of contemplation in the midst of the tranquility of the environmental elements.

Cultural Variety and Solidarity: The Camino is a mixture of societies and foundations. Communicating with pioneers from around the globe encourages a comprehension of variety, separating generalizations and stressing our common humankind. It's an update that in spite of contrasts, we are on a typical excursion.

Community and Fellowship: Explorers share a one of a kind brotherhood brought into the world from a typical reason. Outsiders become associates, offering backing, consolation, and kinship. The shared soul builds up the significance of human association and the worth of a strong local area.

Reflection and Self-Revelation: The isolation of strolling takes into consideration profound reflection. Travelers defy their considerations and feelings, prompting self-revelation. The Camino turns into a figurative mirror mirroring one's feelings of dread, qualities, and the requirement for self-awareness.

Letting Go of Control: The eccentricism of the excursion shows the specialty of giving up. Whether it's unusual climate or changes in plans, the Camino accentuates the worthlessness of attempting to control each part of life. Acknowledgment turns into a key example.

Mindfulness and Presence: Strolling the Camino energizes being available at the time. Each step turns into a contemplation, encouraging care. This training reaches out past the journey, reminding people to see the value in the excursion as opposed to focus on the objective.

Gratitude for Fundamental Necessities: Explorers figure out how to see the value in basic solaces like a hot shower or a warm feast. The shortage of extravagances features the significance of appreciation for essential necessities — an illustration that stretches out to day to day existence.

Arrival and Change: At last arriving at the objective, whether it's Santiago de Compostela or another endpoint, denotes the perfection of the actual excursion. Notwithstanding, the genuine objective is the changed self — an individual who has developed through difficulties, gained from others, and embraced the significant illustrations of the Camino.

Strolling the Camino isn't simply a journey; it's an odyssey of self-revelation, flexibility, and interconnectedness. The illustrations learned on this consecrated excursion become a compass for exploring the multifaceted ways of life, directing people towards individual change and a more profound comprehension of their own reality.

Chapter 10:

Life After the Camino

Returning home and readjusting

The actual fatigue is unmistakable, however it's eclipsed by the psychological and profound restoration that the CAMINO gives. The excursion, frequently embraced as a mission for self-revelation and reflection, leaves explorers with an embroidery of recollections and illustrations. The effortlessness of life on the CAMINO, deprived of current interruptions, cultivates a profound thoughtfulness that stays with you long after the last step.

Getting back, you could wind up wrestling with the unmistakable difference between the serene straightforwardness of the journey and the intricacies of regular daily existence. The test lies in coordinating the examples learned on the CAMINO into your everyday daily practice. The beat of strolling, the brotherhood with individual travelers, and the intelligent isolation become treasured viewpoints that request protection in the midst of the buzzing about of normal life.

The correction stage is a sensitive dance among wistfulness and reality. The bits of knowledge acquired during the journey frequently reshape needs, connections, and points of view. The test isn't only to think back about the CAMINO yet to mix its soul into your everyday presence. This could include taking on a more slow speed, embracing straightforwardness, or encouraging further associations with everyone around you.

The people group fashioned on the CAMINO, a different embroidery of people from different backgrounds, turns into a standard for figuring out the lavishness of human associations. Getting back, keeping up with these associations becomes vital. The bonds shaped during the journey offer a wellspring of solidarity, understanding, and shared encounters that rise above geological limits.

However, correction isn't consistent all the time. The get back can deliver a feeling of removal or an inclination that the individual who left on the CAMINO isn't a similar one returning. This inside shift might prompt a time of thoughtful recalibration, where you adjust your recently discovered comprehension of self to the assumptions and requests of your pre-CAMINO life.

Getting back from the CAMINO isn't simply an actual homecoming however an excursion towards meshing the groundbreaking encounters into the texture of your ordinary reality. It's tied in with protecting the pith of the journey in the midst of the schedules and obligations, making a day to day existence that mirrors the significant examples learned on the way.

How the Camino experience keeps on affecting your life

Joining of Examples Learned: After the Camino, I ended up moving toward difficulties with a newly discovered strength and persistence. The illustration of the long, winding path converted into a commonsense outlook, empowering me to see deterrents as a component of a more extensive excursion. Whether managing work tensions or individual misfortunes, I deliberately applied the Camino's example of persistence.

Adjusted Viewpoints: The Camino ingrained a profound feeling of appreciation for life's basic delights. Indeed, even in the midst of the hustle of everyday schedules, I started valuing the excellence in commonplace minutes — a dawn during my regular drive, a common dinner with family. This change in context enhanced my own insight as well as emphatically affected how I connected with people around me.

Profound Association: Keeping up with the profound association manufactured on the Camino turned into a day to day practice. Normal contemplation and snapshots of calm reflection permitted me to take advantage of a similar feeling of inward harmony experienced during the journey. The Camino's profound pith turned into a directing power, forming my choices and cultivating a feeling of direction.

Proceeded with Connections: The bonds shaped on the Camino ended up being persevering. Month to month video calls with individual explorers turned into an esteemed custom, offering a virtual continuation of the common excursion. The encouraging group of people based on the path developed into a local area that praised achievements, shared difficulties, and gave a consistent sign of the interconnectedness found on the Way.

Appreciation for the Excursion: I began integrating components of the Camino into my regular routine, like going for long strolls in nature. These strolls turned into a custom of care, permitting me to see the value in the actual excursion as opposed to zeroing in exclusively on the objective. The basic demonstration of placing slowly but surely turned into a representation for life's constant development.

Embracing Change: The versatility developed on the Camino appeared in a newly discovered ease with change. Vocation shifts and startling life altering situations were met with a quiet acknowledgment, established in the comprehension that each turn in the way brings its own arrangement of chances and examples. The Camino had changed change from a wellspring of tension to an impetus for development.

Influence on Objectives and Needs: The Camino incited a reconsideration of individual objectives, prompting a more noteworthy accentuation on significant encounters over material pursuits. This change affected choices about profession course, connections, and way of life decisions. The journey had recalibrated my needs, underscoring the significance of association, individual satisfaction, and adding to a more extensive local area.

Proceeding with the Journey in Various Structures: To support the feeling of journey, I laid out a week by week strolling schedule, investigating various paths in my neighborhood. This training filled in as a physical and profound continuation of the Camino. Moreover, captivating in charitable effort inside the neighborhood local area repeated the shared soul of the journey, giving a substantial method for offering in return.

Commitment to Prosperity: The comprehensive effect of the Camino on my prosperity was apparent in better mental and close to home wellbeing. Practices, for example, journaling and offering thanks became necessary to keeping up with balance. The actual work of strolling, enlivened by the everyday journey on the Camino, added to supported actual prosperity.

Motivating Others: Sharing my Camino experience through talks at nearby public venues and online discussions turned into a method for moving others to set out on their own excursions. A few companions and colleagues, dazzled by the extraordinary story, communicated their aim to embrace the journey. Seeing their excitement built up the possibility that the Camino's impact reaches out a long ways past individual encounters.

Chapter 11:

Practical Tips and Resources

Advice for future pilgrims

Research Your Route: Understand the route you'll be taking for the pilgrimage. Familiarize yourself with key stops, distances, and terrain.

Physical Preparation: Start a fitness regimen well in advance. Pilgrimages often involve long walks, so build your stamina gradually.

Appropriate Footwear: Invest in comfortable, well-fitting hiking boots. Break them in before the pilgrimage to avoid blisters.

Weather Considerations: Check the weather conditions for your pilgrimage period and pack accordingly. Be prepared for unexpected changes.

Packing Essentials:

Lightweight Backpack: Choose a backpack that distributes weight evenly and has adjustable straps for comfort.

Clothing: Pack layers suitable for various weather conditions. Include a rainproof jacket and quick-drying clothes.

First Aid Kit: Carry basic medical supplies – bandages, pain relievers, blister pads, and any personal medications.

Navigation Tools: Have a reliable map, compass, or GPS device. Familiarize yourself with navigation apps tailored for pilgrims.

Cultural and Spiritual Aspects:

Respect Local Customs: Learn about the cultural norms of the regions you'll be passing through and be respectful.

Connect with Locals: Engage with the local community to enhance your cultural experience. Share stories and listen to theirs.

Spiritual Preparation: Reflect on the spiritual significance of the pilgrimage. Consider incorporating meditation or prayer into your routine.

Logistical Considerations:

Accommodations: Research and book accommodations in advance. Pilgrimage routes can get crowded, especially during peak times.

Budgeting: Estimate costs for accommodations, meals, and any unforeseen expenses. Have a contingency fund. Emergency Contacts: Carry a list of emergency contacts, including local authorities and embassy information.

Health and Well-being:

Hydration:Stay well-hydrated, especially during long walks. Carry a reusable water bottle.

Rest and Recovery: Listen to your body. Take breaks when needed, and ensure you get enough rest each night.

Mindfulness Practices: Incorporate mindfulness practices into your journey. This can include daily reflections or gratitude exercises.

Post-Pilgrimage Reflection:

Journaling: Keep a journal to document your experiences, thoughts, and emotions throughout the pilgrimage.

Community Engagement: Stay connected with fellow pilgrims post-journey. Share insights and support each other's post-pilgrimage reflections.

Integration: Consider how the pilgrimage has influenced your life. Integrate lessons learned into your daily routine.

Recommended Resources:

Guidebooks: Invest in guidebooks specific to your pilgrimage route for detailed information and insights.

Online Forums: Join online forums or social media groups where past and future pilgrims share tips and experiences.

Pilgrimage Organizations: Connect with pilgrimage organizations that can provide support, guidance, and additional resources. Remember, each pilgrimage is a unique journey. Embrace the challenges and joys, stay open to unexpected experiences, and savor the transformative power of the pilgrimage. Safe travels!

Chapter 12:

Itinerary in Camino

14 days itinerary in Camino Francés

Day 1: Saint-Jean-Pied-de-Port to Roncesvalles: Start your journey in Saint-Jean-Pied-de-Port, a picturesque French town. The first day involves a challenging ascent over the Pyrenees, leading you to Roncesvalles in Spain. The scenery is breathtaking, and you'll cover around 25 kilometers.

Day 2: Roncesvalles to Zubiri: From Roncesvalles, the Camino continues through lush landscapes and charming villages. Zubiri, around 22 kilometers from Roncesvalles, provides a welcoming stop for the night.

Day 3: Zubiri to Pamplona: Walk through the scenic countryside and arrive in Pamplona, famous for its Running of the Bulls festival. This day covers approximately 21 kilometers.

Day 4: Pamplona to Puente la Reina: Leaving Pamplona, you'll pass through vineyards and small villages, eventually reaching Puente la Reina, a town with a historic bridge. The distance is around 24 kilometers.

Day 5: Puente la Reina to Estella: The trail takes you through vineyards and olive groves, leading to Estella. Enjoy the rich history of this town after walking approximately 22 kilometers.

Day 6: Estella to Los Arcos: Pass through picturesque landscapes and charming towns like Villamayor de Monjardín on your way to Los Arcos, covering about 21 kilometers.

Day 7: Los Arcos to Logroño: Today's journey leads to Logroño, known for its excellent wines. The distance is around 27 kilometers, and you'll cross the famous wine region of La Rioja.

Day 8: Logroño to Nájera: Continue through vineyards and small villages, reaching Nájera after approximately 30 kilometers. Explore the town's historical sites and unwind.

Day 9: Nájera to Santo Domingo de la Calzada: Traverse vineyards and rolling hills to Santo Domingo de la Calzada. This stage covers about 21 kilometers.

Day 10: Santo Domingo de la Calzada to Belorado: Pass through expansive farmlands and charming hamlets on your way to Belorado, covering approximately 22 kilometers.

Day 11: Belorado to San Juan de Ortega: Experience the tranquility of rural landscapes as you head towards San Juan de Ortega, walking around 24 kilometers.

Day 12: San Juan de Ortega to Burgos: Arrive in Burgos, a city with a rich cultural heritage. The day's journey is around 26 kilometers.

Day 13: Burgos to Hontanas: Walk through the Meseta, a vast plateau, and reach Hontanas after covering approximately 31 kilometers.

Day 14: Hontanas to Boadilla del Camino: Your final day involves walking through vast plains to Boadilla del Camino, where you can reflect on your pilgrimage. The distance is around 28 kilometers.

Adjustments to daily distances can be made based on individual preferences and physical condition. Always check the latest guidebooks or local information for any route changes or recommendations. Enjoy your transformative journey on the Camino Francés!

14 day Itinerary in Camino Portugués

Day 1: Lisbon to Alverca do Ribatejo: Begin your Camino Portugués venture in Lisbon and advance toward Alverca do Ribatejo. This underlying stage covers around 32 kilometers and incorporates a blend of metropolitan and riverside strolling.

Day 2: Alverca do Ribatejo to Azambuja: Go on through picturesque scenes, passing grape plantations and unassuming communities, to arrive at Azambuja. This day's walk is roughly 20 kilometers.

Day 3: Azambuja to Santarém::Stroll through country regions and noteworthy towns, showing up in Santarém subsequent to covering around 33 kilometers. Santarém offers a rich verifiable encounter.

Day 4: Santarém to Golegã: The path takes you through pleasant scenes and farmlands to Golegã. This stage is around 30 kilometers.

Day 5: Golegã to Tomar: Go through olive forests and eucalyptus woods, arriving at Tomar after around 33 kilometers. Tomar is known for its Knight Palace and Religious circle of Christ.

Day 6: Tomar to Alvaiázere: Stroll through woodlands and enchanting towns, showing up in Alvaiázere in the wake of covering around 31 kilometers.

Day 7: Alvaiázere to Rabaçal: Proceed with your excursion through the Portuguese open country, tiny villas en route to Rabaçal. This stage is around 22 kilometers.

Day 8: Rabaçal to Coimbra: The path leads you through forests and farmlands, arriving at Coimbra in the wake of strolling around 31 kilometers. Investigate the notable city and its college.

Day 9: Coimbra to Mealhada: Go through grape plantations and rich scenes, showing up in Mealhada subsequent to covering roughly 22 kilometers.

Day 10: Mealhada to Águeda: Stroll through rustic landscape and little towns to arrive at Águeda. This day's distance is around 24 kilometers.

Day 11: Águeda to Albergaria-a-Nova: Proceed with your excursion through pleasant scenes and show up in Albergaria-a-Nova in the wake of strolling roughly 19 kilometers.

Day 12: Albergaria-a-Nova to São João de Madeira: Stroll through assorted scenes, including woodlands and metropolitan regions, arriving at São João de Madeira subsequent to covering around 24 kilometers.

Day 13: São João de Madeira to Porto: The last stretch takes you to the energetic city of Porto, covering around 33 kilometers. Investigate the memorable city and commend the fruition of your journey.

Day 14: Rest day in Porto: Take a merited rest in Porto, investigating its rich history, flavorful cooking, and picturesque riverside. Think about your Camino Portugués venture and partake in the city's social contributions.

Change the everyday distances in light of your speed and inclinations, and consistently check for refreshed trail data. Safe goes on your Camino Portugués experience!

14 days itinerary in Camino del Norte

Day 1: Irún to San Sebastián: Set out on your Camino del Norte experience in Irún, strolling along the northern bank of Spain to the beautiful city of San Sebastián. The primary day covers roughly 28 kilometers, offering staggering waterfront sees.

Day 2: San Sebastián to Zarautz: Proceed with the coast, going through beguiling fishing towns. Show up in Zarautz subsequent to strolling around 21 kilometers, and partake in the town's wonderful ocean side.

Day 3: Zarautz to Deba: The path leads you through moving slopes and beach front scenes to Deba, covering around 22 kilometers. Take in the beautiful excellence and coastline climate.

Day 4: Deba to Markina-Xemein: Stroll through assorted scenes, including woods and provincial regions, arriving at Markina-Xemein after roughly 26 kilometers.

Day 5: Markina-Xemein to Gernika-Lumo: Navigate the Basque open country and show up in Gernika-Lumo, known for its authentic importance. This stage covers around 24 kilometers.

Day 6: Gernika-Lumo to Lezama: Proceed with your excursion through the Basque district, going through towns and farmlands to arrive at Lezama subsequent to strolling around 27 kilometers.

Day 7: Lezama to Bilbao: Stroll to Bilbao, an energetic city with a blend of present day and noteworthy attractions. This day's distance is around 11 kilometers, permitting time to investigate Bilbao's Guggenheim Gallery and different milestones.

Day 8: Bilbao to Pobeña: The path takes you along the coast and through modern regions, arriving at Pobeña in the wake of covering around 25 kilometers.

Day 9: Pobeña to Castro-Urdiales: Proceed with the northern coast, passing bluffs and sea shores, and show up in Castro-Urdiales in the wake of strolling roughly 28 kilometers.

Day 10: Castro-Urdiales to Laredo: Stroll along the shore and through ocean side towns to arrive at Laredo subsequent to covering around 26 kilometers. Partake in the sea shores and notable locales.

Day 11: Laredo to Güemes: The path leads you through scenes of fields and towns to Güemes, covering roughly 32 kilometers. Güemes is known for its albergue and inviting air.

Day 12: Güemes to Santander: Proceed with the coast to Santander, a dynamic city with lovely sea shores. This day's distance is around 20 kilometers, permitting time to investigate Santander's attractions.

Day 13: Santander to Santillana del Blemish: Stroll through beautiful wide open to Santillana del Blemish, known for its all around saved archaic design. This stage covers around 38 kilometers.

Day 14: Santillana del Blemish to Comillas: Close your Camino del Norte venture in Comillas, strolling around 23 kilometers. Investigate the town's memorable structures and loosen up in the wake of finishing this northern beach front journey.

Change everyday distances in view of your speed and inclinations, and consistently check for refreshed trail data. Buen Camino on your Camino del Norte!

14 days itinerary in the Camino Primitivo.

The Camino Primitivo is a noteworthy and more uncommon course of the Camino de Santiago, offering an extraordinary and testing journey insight. Here is a nitty gritty 14-day Itinerary:

Day 1: Oviedo: Begin your excursion in Oviedo, the capital of Asturias. Visit the Oviedo Church and San Salvador House of prayer. Investigate the notable old town and appreciate neighborhood cooking.

Day 2: Oviedo to Grado (25 km) Start your Camino Primitivo by strolling to Grado. Go through rich scenes and beguiling towns. Visit the Congregation of San Juan in Grado.

Day 3: Grado to Salas (20 km) Proceed with your excursion through pleasant open country. Investigate the archaic town of Salas and its palace.

Day 4: Salas to Tineo (20 km) Journey across timberlands and moving slopes. Arrive at Tineo and visit the Congregation of St Nick Maria.

Day 5: Tineo to Borres (24 km) Experience the changing scenes as you stroll to Borres. Partake in the serenity of the provincial environmental factors.

Day 6: Borres to Berducedo (17 km) Go through enchanting villages and cross antiquated spans. Show up in Berducedo, a little town with a serene environment.

Day 7: Berducedo to Grandas de Salime (25 km) Stroll through thick timberlands and cross the Grandas de Salime supply. Investigate Grandas de Salime and its ethnographic exhibition hall.

Day 8: Grandas de Salime to Fonsagrada (22 km) Navigate through timberlands and open scenes. Arrive at Fonsagrada, a town with a rich social legacy.

Day 9: Fonsagrada to O Cadavo (27 km) Venture through undulating landscape and calm towns. Investigate O Cadavo and its authentic locales.

Day 10: O Cadavo to Lugo (30 km) Stroll through woods and fields prior to showing up in Lugo. Visit Lugo's Roman walls, an UNESCO World Legacy site.

Day 11: Lugo to Ferreira (29 km) Investigate Lugo in the first part of the day and begin your stroll to Ferreira. Go through little towns and partake in the provincial view.

Day 12: Ferreira to Melide (26 km) Stroll through eucalyptus backwoods and farmland. Arrive at Melide and appreciate the nearby forte, octopus.

Day 13: Melide to Arzúa (14 km) A more limited day of strolling, permitting time to investigate Arzúa. Visit the Congregation of St Nick María and partake in the nearby cooking.

Day 14: Arzúa to Santiago de Compostela (39 km)The last stretch to Santiago de Compostela. Show up in the early evening and visit the House of prayer of Santiago.

This schedule gives an equilibrium of strolling distances, social encounters, and normal magnificence, offering a satisfying excursion along the Camino Primitivo. Changes can be made in view of individual inclinations and actual abilities.

Printed by Amazon Italia Logistica S.r.l.
Torrazza Piemonte (TO), Italy

56397346R00077